Mountain Rescue

Written by Cynthia Rider
based on the original characters
created by Roderick Hunt and Alex Brychta
Illustrated by Alex Brychta

OXFORD
UNIVERSITY PRESS

Biff was showing Wilma her new
music box.

"It's like a little house," said Wilma.

Biff opened the box and the music
began to play. Suddenly, the magic
key began to glow.

The magic took Biff and Wilma
to a mountain railway station.

"The station looks just like my
music box," said Biff.

There was a big wooden horn
at the station. A boy called Max told
them that it was used to send for the
Mountain Rescue helicopter.

"My Uncle Hans flies the helicopter," he said. "He's taking me to see an eagle's nest today. You can come with us."

9

The children got into a train. It took them higher up the mountain. Uncle Hans was waiting at the station.

"Hi Max," said Uncle Hans. "I'm
glad some of your friends have
come with you."

Uncle Hans and the children went
up a steep track. They saw some
people climbing a steep rock.

"That looks scary!" said Biff.

Just then, Uncle Hans's phone rang. "I have to go back, but you can see the eagle's nest from here," he said.

The eagle was sitting on her nest.
Suddenly, she squawked and flew
into the sky.

"A man has climbed up to the nest!" said Biff. "He's putting the eagle's egg into his bag."

"Put that egg back!" shouted
Wilma.

The man looked up. He saw the
children watching him and started
to run.

"He's going to the station," said
Max. "Quick! Let's follow him and
get the egg back." They slipped and
scrambled down the steep path.

At last, they reached the station.
Wilma ran up to the man.

"We saw you take an egg from the
eagle's nest," she said.

The man was angry. "I didn't take
an egg," he said, and he opened his
bag. There was no egg inside.

Suddenly, there was a shout.

"One of the climbers has fallen!"
said Max. "We must call the
Mountain Rescue Team."

Wilma ran to blow the horn, but
the man tried to stop her.

"Give me that horn!" he shouted,
but Wilma pulled it away from him.

Wilma looked in the horn. "He's
hidden the egg in here!" she said.

The man started to run but Biff
tripped him up . . . CRASH!

Max took the egg and wrapped it
in his jacket to keep it warm.

Then Wilma blew the horn.

BOOM! . . . BOOM! . . . BOOM!

The Mountain Rescue helicopter
flew into the sky. Everyone cheered
as the climber was lifted to safety.

The helicopter landed and Max
showed Uncle Hans the eagle's egg.
  "We must put the egg back before
it gets cold," said Uncle Hans.

Uncle Hans climbed up to the nest
and put the egg back. The eagle saw
the egg and flew back to her nest.

Three big feathers floated gently
down to the children.

"The eagle is saying thank you,"
said Biff, as the magic key glowed.

"Look! There's a wooden horn
on your music box now," said
Wilma. "How did it get there?"
"It must be magic," smiled Biff.

Talk about the story

What was the big wooden horn used for?

How do you think the children felt when the man showed them his empty bag?

Why did Max wrap the egg in his jacket?

How would you feel if you saw someone steal something?

A maze

Help Uncle Hans put the egg back.